40 Days with
The Gospel of Mark

A 40-Day Biblical
Devotional Journal:
Study • Reflect • Discern • Pray

40 Days With…The Gospel of Mark
A 40-Day Biblical Devotional Journal: Study Reflect Discern Pray

PREFACE

As a pastor, I am a big fan of daily devotions. Dedicated time reflecting on Scripture helps me grow in my faith and often helps me keep my daily life in a proper perspective. I have used many different devotionals through the years. This series of devotionals was developed in an attempt to address a few shortcomings I have encountered in devotionals currently available.

- Many devotionals are 365 days. Sometimes, I simply cannot or do not want to make a 365 day commitment to one devotional. Sometimes I want or need to focus my devotion time in another direction for a season – for example, maybe I want to use an Advent devotional. Sometimes, I fall behind a few days and then it becomes a chore to catch up, or I skip the missed days and might lose some of the intended devotional continuity.

- Many devotionals offer a scripture accompanied by the thoughts and relevant stories of the author. While these are frequently insightful and inspirational, the author's voice is primary. My attention drifts away too easily from the Scripture to the author's thoughts and stories. I want a devotional that keeps the Scripture primary and helps me create space for God to talk to me through the Scripture of the day. I want to listen for what God is saying to me...today...in this Scripture.

- Many devotionals jump around from one favorite scripture to the next. Again, these individual daily devotionals may be inspiring and helpful. However, encountering these scriptures out of context may make it difficult to see the "big picture" of the story of God. I want a devotional that allows me to encounter the Scripture within the larger context in which it is found. When you complete a *40 Days With…* devotional, you will gain a familiarity with the subject of that volume.

Additionally, I want to intentionally reflect on what I'm learning and discerning from my daily encounter with Scripture. For these reasons, my *40 Days With…* devotionals will be both devotional and journal. My hope is that you will find this hybrid approach to devotionals to be a helpful resource in your spiritual life. Every 40 days you can immerse yourself in a fresh scriptural devotional.

About the Editor

Rev. Chris Barbieri is an ordained Deacon in the United Methodist Church living in Georgia and serving in the North Georgia Conference. Chris is a recognized leader in the area of adult spiritual formation and church leadership. He serves through Digital Deacon Ministries, LLC as an author and consultant. He enjoys leading studies and small groups and his signature workshop is "Better Bible Teaching Starts Now!" Chris also serves on various leadership boards in his community.

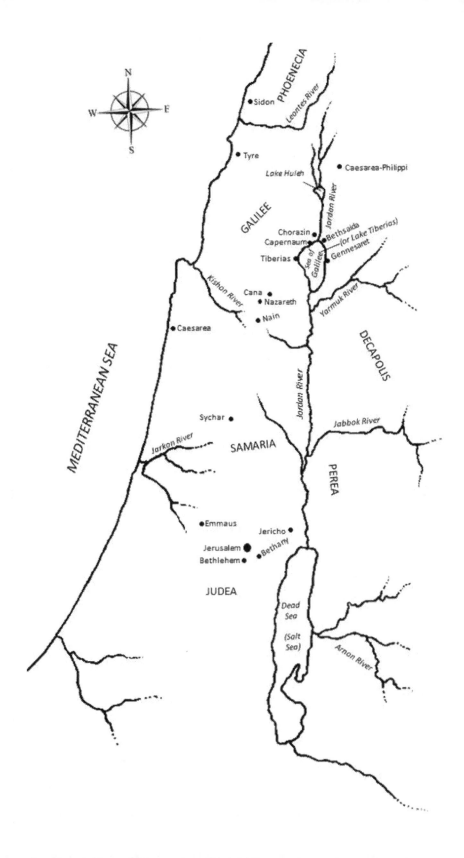

HOW TO USE THIS DEVOTIONAL

Lectio Divina is an ancient practice of the church in which Christians "prayed the scriptures." Individually or in small groups, a passage of scripture was read three or four times – with silence in between each reading. We should remember that very few people could read in the early church and most people encountered scripture by hearing it. Participants listened carefully, not so they could "learn" in an academic sense. Rather, they listened for how God might be speaking to them in that moment. The ***40 Days With...*** devotionals are designed such that you might listen for God's voice in each day's message in a similar manner.

Know that you will likely get what you put into these devotionals. If you hurry through the reading so you can check it off your to-do list, do not expect many insights or spiritual growth.

As with all devotionals, first find a quiet place free of any distractions. Ideally, you will have a regular place for your devotional time. Plan on spending 15-30 minutes on the devotional pages for the day.

1) Pray – Ask God to clear your mind of the mental clutter and invite the Holy Spirit to speak to you.

2) Turn to your current day's devotional pages.

3) Read the passage slowly and carefully.

4) If possible, read it aloud to yourself a second time.

5) First ask yourself if any words or phrases stand out to you. Don't worry about making sense of them. Simply note these words. Each page has a designated space for you to note these words and phrases.

6) Read the passage again (either silently or aloud, as you prefer.)

7) Reflect on the passage in silence. Do you have any insights? How does this passage apply to you…today? Has this passage put something on your "radar?" Has an image popped in your head as you've reflected? Did this passage raise a question in your mind? Do you particularly identify with anyone in the passage? What emotions are present in the passage? What emotions do you feel as you read the passage?

8) Take 5-10 minutes to write down any thoughts you have had during your time of reflection. Each passage has blank space to record your insights, thoughts, and questions.

9) Read the passage one last time. In this final reading, ask yourself if you feel God calling you to any particular action. Record any additional thoughts you may have.

10) Turn back to the front of the devotional and find the index pages. Find the entry for today's passage. In the "Key Phrase" box, write down the main phrase that you focused on from today's passage. In the "Key Insight" box, try to summarize your thoughts on the passage in one or two sentences.

The first few pages of each devotional volume will serve as an index. You will complete the day's index entry AFTER you have completed the daily devotional pages. In the future, the index may help you reference your insights on a particular passage. You may find it beneficial to periodically review the index pages of a completed devotional.

Know that the Bible is more of a library than a single book. It contains many different books by many different authors. Even within the books, different kinds of scripture are encountered. The Gospels contain a mixture of narrative, teaching, and miracle episodes. The Psalms are poetry and Paul's writings are letters.

The narrative sections may not seem as inspiring as one of Jesus' parables, but these sections are important. They connect the story and help us see where Jesus is and to whom he his is speaking. One of the goals of these devotionals is to help you increase your familiarity with your Bible.

On some days you may be overwhelmed with insights about something Jesus taught. You may feel you need more space to write than the devotional provides. On another day, the scripture may tell the story of Jesus moving from point A to point B and you may not discern any major insights. However, knowing that Jesus moved from A to B might inform the next day's reading. Do not worry about how much or little you hear or write on each day. Simply embrace the process of this daily immersion in Scripture.

Why the Common English Bible Translation Was Chosen

The Common English Bible (CEB) is the most recent English language scholarly translation of the Bible and was published in 2011. The CEB was a cooperative project involving the Disciples of Christ, Presbyterian Church USA, Episcopal Church, United Church of Christ, and United Methodist Church. Several leading Catholic scholars also participated in this project.

An explicit aim of this project was to produce an easily readable English translation. The editors struck a balance between faithful translation of the original ancient texts and readability.

The CEB is a translation, meaning it originates from ancient texts in their original languages. Many "modern" English Bibles are paraphrases in which the editors may or may not take a good deal of interpretive license in translating passages. While paraphrase Bibles can be useful, I have intentionally chosen an English translation which faithfully adhered to strict standards in translating the original Biblical texts.

I have chosen the CEB because:

1) It is the most current translation. I personally know some of the translation editors who worked on this project and I know it was well done.

2) As the newest English translation, many readers will not be familiar with it. Readers are likely to slow down and pay closer attention as they read the CEB. When we slow down and focus on the Scriptures, we make more room for the Holy Spirit to speak us. My hope is that this relatively fresh translation will let you experience the Bible in a fresh way.

Feel free to use another translation if you would like. For ease of use, I wanted to have everything you needed for quality devotional time in one volume. One of the barriers in my own devotional life is I get frustrated when I'm trying to hold a devotional journal steady, balance a Bible (or smartphone/tablet with a Bible app), and try to write something legible. These devotionals are designed such that all you need is a pen and a quiet place.

More on Translating the Bible

Translating ancient Greek, Hebrew, and Aramaic is not always a straightforward matter. Some passages are notoriously difficult to translate. Also, our modern Bible did not originate as a "single scroll" that was passed down through the centuries. Rather, there are dozens and dozens of scrolls, fragments, and manuscripts that have come down to us through history. These scrolls do not always agree with one another. Determining which version of a passage is most likely the "original" is a challenging scholarly exercise. Early English translators were not aware of many of these challenging translation issues, resulting in noticeable differences in some passages.

For example, there is a "short ending" and a "long ending" to the book of Mark. Most modern scholars agree that the long ending (verses 9-20) was added in the second century. Any good study Bible will point out these finer points of translation in a footnote.

In the CEB, you will occasionally notice a break in sequence between verse numbers. Most of the time, these breaks mean the translation editors believe the missing verses were not a part of the original Biblical text.

USING THIS DEVOTIONAL AS A SMALL GROUP RESOURCE

In addition to using this devotional as a personal study resource, you may wish to use it in a small group setting. You will find it easy to adapt *40 Days with...* books for use as a 6-week resource in a small group. (Your last week will only have 5 days of material.) Two possible formats for this are offered below. Feel free to develop your own format that fits your setting.

Option 1

1) Agree with all study participants on a common start date and ensure everyone has a copy of the devotional.

2) Meet weekly at an agreed upon time and place for 1 hour to 1 hour and 30 minutes.

3) Identify a facilitator and a prayer leader for each week. The prayer leader will open and close the group with prayer. The facilitator will read the scripture and the guiding questions. So that different voices are part of the experience, the facilitator and prayer leader will not be the same person any given week. You may choose to

rotate responsibilities in your group or have one person designated for each role for your small group.

4) You may wish to use this as a template for your sessions:

- Welcome and opening prayer (5 minutes)

- Spend 5-10 minutes on the prior 6 days' of devotional scripture readings. For each, the facilitator should first ask what words or phrases did people note. Then ask if anyone felt called to any particular action or has an insight to share. If anyone felt called to an action, you may wish to ask the person if he/she would like the group to hold him/her accountable. If so, note this and be sure to ask the person about the action in following weeks. (5 minutes per scripture = 30 minutes, 10 minutes per scripture = 60 minutes)

- Spend 20 minutes experiencing the current day's scripture in *Lectio Divina* style.

  - Begin with 30 seconds of silence for everyone to clear their minds.

  - The facilitator should read the scripture. Then allow 30 seconds of silence.

  - Facilitator say: "Hear the scripture again. Listen for words or phrases that catch your attention." Read the scripture again. Allow 30 seconds of silence. Ask participants to note any key words or phrases in the journal section of the book.

  - Facilitator invites everyone to close their eyes and hear the scripture a third time. Read the scripture again. Allow 15 seconds of silence. Pause 15-20 seconds between each question below.

1. Ask: What emotions are present in the passage?

2. Ask: Did you identify with anyone in particular in the passage?

3. Ask: Did you feel any particular emotions as you heard the passage?

4. Ask: Has an image popped into your mind as you heard the passage?

5. Ask: How does this passage apply to you…today?

□ Invite participants to take a few minutes to record their thoughts in the journal.

□ Facilitator say: "Hear the scripture one last time. Do you feel God calling you to some specific action in this passage?" Read the scripture again. Invite people to record any final thoughts.

• Take prayer requests and offer closing prayer (10-15 minutes)

• [Note: You may wish to preview each week's scripture and pre-select one for this *Lectio Divina* experience. It's possible that the group might find one day's scripture more 'interesting' than the seventh day scripture. If you opt for this, be sure to communicate this plan to everyone in your group.]

Option 2

1) Agree with all study participants on a common start date and ensure everyone has a copy of the devotional.

2) Meet weekly at an agreed upon time and place for 1 hour 30 minutes.

3) Rotate responsibility for opening and closing the group with prayer. Use a signup sheet if you wish or simply share the responsibility informally.

4) You may wish to use this as a template for your sessions:

- Welcome and opening prayer (5 minutes)

- Spend approximately 10 minutes on the prior seven days' of devotional scripture readings. For each, the facilitator should first ask what words or phrases did people note. Then ask if anyone felt called to any particular action or has an insight to share. If anyone felt called to an action, you may wish to ask the person if he/she would like the group to hold him/her accountable. If so, note this and be sure to ask the person about the action in following weeks. (10 minutes per scripture = 70 minutes)

- Take prayer requests and offer closing prayer (10-15 minutes)

INTRODUCTION TO THE GOSPEL OF MARK

Most scholars accept that the Gospel of Mark was the first gospel written and generally agree on a date of approximately 70 C.E. We must remember that most people in the first century could not read and the stories of Jesus and his ministry were initially shared orally through stories. We refer to this as "oral tradition." A few decades after Jesus' death and resurrection, the early church seemed to recognize the need to write down the stories of Jesus' ministry. The first generation of Jesus followers were likely dying out and the author of Mark was an early 'historian' who sought to capture these stories before this first generation died.

The Gospel of Mark is the shortest of the gospels and is only about 60 percent the length of the Gospel of Matthew. Scholars disagree as to whether the author of Mark, a common name of the period, is the same Mark mentioned as a companion with Paul. The author focuses primarily on the miraculous signs of Jesus, which establish the authority of Jesus. The author clearly wants us to know Jesus possesses the power and authority of God. Little sense of time and location is shared and gives the gospel a loosely connected narrative style. Because of the brevity of Mark, you will study the majority of Mark by completing this devotional volume.

The author sets a frenetic pace in telling the story of Jesus. The story of John the Baptist, Jesus' baptism, and Jesus' temptation all occur in the first 16 verses. Transitions between episodes are brief or non-existent, especially when compared with the style of Matthew or Luke. Luke takes nearly 10 chapters to tell the story of Jesus' final journey from Galilee to Jerusalem. The author of Mark makes this journey in one verse. Indeed, the author simply uses "Immediately" more than 40 times to connect episodes in Jesus' ministry. Thus, in Mark's gospel, the 'who' and 'what' are emphasized and the 'when' and 'where' are de-emphasized.

The miracles of Jesus are front and center in the Gospel of Mark. Again, the author wants us to be clear that Jesus has the power and authority of God. Jesus frequently challenges the normal conventions of his day. Because the miracles have established Jesus' authority, he is now a credible teacher in his parables. Interestingly, Mark does not refer to Jesus as the Son of God. Rather, he is most often called the Son of Man in this gospel.

In spite of the many miracles performed by Jesus, his disciples struggle to grasp the true identity of Jesus as Messiah. They are "blind" to who Jesus is, even as many outsiders "see" and recognize Jesus as Messiah. We witness first hand that discipleship with Jesus is not easy. Sometimes we see Jesus transparently and at other times seeing Jesus can be elusive.

Devotional Start Date: _____

Day 1	Mark 1:1-8	Key phrase
Key Insight		

Day 2	Mark 1:16-21	Key phrase
Key Insight		

Day 3	Mark 1:22-28	Key phrase
Key Insight		

Day 4	Mark 1:29-39	Key phrase
Key Insight		

Day 5	Mark 2:1-12	Key phrase
Key Insight		

Day 6	Mark 2:23-28	Key phrase
Key Insight		

Day 7	Mark 3:1-6	Key phrase
Key Insight		

Day 8	Mark 4:1-9,13-20	Key phrase
Key Insight		

Day 9	Mark 4:21-34	Key phrase
Key Insight		

Day 10	Mark 4:35-41	Key phrase
Key Insight		

Day 11	Mark 5:21-24, 35-43	Key phrase
Key Insight		

Day 12	Mark 6:30-44	Key phrase
Key Insight		

Day 13	Mark 7:1-13	Key phrase
Key Insight		

Day 14	Mark 7:14-23	Key phrase
Key Insight		

Day 15	Mark 7:31-37	Key phrase
Key Insight		

Day 16	Mark 8:1-10	Key phrase

Key Insight

Day 17	Mark 8:22-26	Key phrase

Key Insight

Day 18	Mark 8:27-38	Key phrase

Key Insight

Day 19	Mark 9:2-10	Key phrase

Key Insight

Day 20	Mark 9:14-29	Key phrase

Key Insight

Day 21	Mark 9:33-37, 42-43, 45, 47-49	Key phrase
Key Insight		

Day 22	Mark 10:17-31	Key phrase
Key Insight		

Day 23	Mark 10:35-45	Key phrase
Key Insight		

Day 24	Mark 10:46-52	Key phrase
Key Insight		

Day 25	Mark 11:1-11	Key phrase
Key Insight		

Day 26	Mark 11:15-19	Key phrase

Key Insight

Day 27	Mark 12:1-12	Key phrase

Key Insight

Day 28	Mark 12:13-17	Key phrase

Key Insight

Day 29	Mark 12:28-34	Key phrase

Key Insight

Day 30	Mark 12:38-44	Key phrase

Key Insight

Day 31	Mark 13:28-37	Key phrase

Key Insight

Day 32	Mark 14:3-9	Key phrase

Key Insight

Day 33	Mark 14:12-26	Key phrase

Key Insight

Day 34	Mark 14:32-42	Key phrase

Key Insight

Day 35	Mark 14:53-65	Key phrase

Key Insight

Day 36	Mark 14:27-31, 66-72	Key phrase
Key Insight		

Day 37	Mark 15:6-15, 21-32	Key phrase
Key Insight		

Day 38	Mark 15:33-41	Key phrase
Key Insight		

Day 39	Mark 15:42-16:8	Key phrase
Key Insight		

Day 40	Mark 16:9-20	Key phrase
Key Insight		

One Final Thought...

If you are familiar with the day's passage, avoid the trap of rushing through it. I believe the Holy Spirit speaks to us through Scripture if we allow the proper time and space. Too often when we encounter a familiar Scripture, we allow our minds to rush to the end ("Oh yeah… I know how this parable ends"). Our minds turn away from Scripture to our normal mental clutter. As you progress through the devotional, avoid this trap and listen carefully to what the Scripture is saying to you today. Try to erase any preconceptions about the passage and approach it with fresh eyes and ears. I have found this practice to be incredibly fruitful in my own personal study. I notice things I never noticed before and I hear things I've missed over and over in prior readings.

Mark 1:1-8

1 The beginning of the good news about Jesus Christ, God's Son, 2 happened just as it was written about in the prophecy of Isaiah:

Look, I am sending my messenger before you.

He will prepare your way,

3 a voice shouting in the wilderness:
"Prepare the way for the Lord;
make his paths straight."

4 John the Baptist was in the wilderness calling for people to be baptized to show that they were changing their hearts and lives and wanted God to forgive their sins.

5 Everyone in Judea and all the people of Jerusalem went out to the Jordan River and were being baptized by John as they confessed their sins.

6 John wore clothes made of camel's hair, with a leather belt around his waist. He ate locusts and wild honey.

7 He announced, "One stronger than I am is coming after me. I'm not even worthy to bend over and loosen the strap of his sandals.

8 I baptize you with water, but he will baptize you with the Holy Spirit."

Key words or phrases?

Insights?

Mark 1:16-21

16 As Jesus passed alongside the Galilee Sea, he saw two brothers, Simon and Andrew, throwing fishing nets into the sea, for they were fishermen.

17 "Come, follow me," he said, "and I'll show you how to fish for people."

18 Right away, they left their nets and followed him.

19 After going a little farther, he saw James and John, Zebedee's sons, in their boat repairing the fishing nets.

20 At that very moment he called them. They followed him, leaving their father Zebedee in the boat with the hired workers.

21 Jesus and his followers went into Capernaum. Immediately on the Sabbath Jesus entered the synagogue and started teaching.

Key words or phrases?

Insights?

Mark 1:22-28

22 The people were amazed by his teaching, for he was teaching them with authority, not like the legal experts.

23 Suddenly, there in the synagogue, a person with an evil spirit screamed, 24 "What have you to do with us, Jesus of Nazareth? Have you come to destroy us? I know who you are. You are the holy one from God."

25 "Silence!" Jesus said, speaking harshly to the demon. "Come out of him!"

26 The unclean spirit shook him and screamed, then it came out.

27 Everyone was shaken and questioned among themselves, "What's this? A new teaching with authority! He even commands unclean spirits and they obey him!"

28 Right away the news about him spread throughout the entire region of Galilee.

Key words or phrases?

Insights?

Mark 1:29-39

²⁹ After leaving the synagogue, Jesus, James, and John went home with Simon and Andrew.

³⁰ Simon's mother-in-law was in bed, sick with a fever, and they told Jesus about her at once.

³¹ He went to her, took her by the hand, and raised her up. The fever left her, and she served them.

³² That evening, at sunset, people brought to Jesus those who were sick or demon-possessed.

³³ The whole town gathered near the door.

³⁴ He healed many who were sick with all kinds of diseases, and he threw out many demons. But he didn't let the demons speak, because they recognized him.

³⁵ Early in the morning, well before sunrise, Jesus rose and went to a deserted place where he could be alone in prayer.

³⁶ Simon and those with him tracked him down.

³⁷ When they found him, they told him, "Everyone's looking for you!"

³⁸ He replied, "Let's head in the other direction, to the nearby villages, so that I can preach there too. That's why I've come."

³⁹ He traveled throughout Galilee, preaching in their synagogues and throwing out demons.

Key words or phrases?

Insights?

Mark 2:1-12

1   After a few days, Jesus went back to Capernaum, and people heard that he was at home.

2   So many gathered that there was no longer space, not even near the door. Jesus was speaking the word to them.

3   Some people arrived, and four of them were bringing to him a man who was paralyzed.

4   They couldn't carry him through the crowd, so they tore off part of the roof above where Jesus was. When they had made an opening, they lowered the mat on which the paralyzed man was lying.

5   When Jesus saw their faith, he said to the paralytic, "Child, your sins are forgiven!"

6   Some legal experts were sitting there, muttering among themselves, 7 "Why does he speak this way? He's insulting God. Only the one God can forgive sins."

8   Jesus immediately recognized what they were discussing, and he said to them, "Why do you fill your minds with these questions?

9   Which is easier—to say to a paralyzed person, 'Your sins are forgiven,' or to say, 'Get up, take up your bed, and walk'?

10   But so you will know that the Human One has authority on the earth to forgive sins"—he said to the man who was paralyzed, 11 "Get up, take your mat, and go home."

12   Jesus raised him up, and right away he picked up his mat and walked out in front of everybody. They were all amazed and praised God, saying, "We've never seen anything like this!"

Key words or phrases?

Insights?

Mark 2:23-28

23 Jesus went through the wheat fields on the Sabbath. As the disciples made their way, they were picking the heads of wheat.

24 The Pharisees said to Jesus, "Look! Why are they breaking the Sabbath law?"

25 He said to them, "Haven't you ever read what David did when he was in need, when he and those with him were hungry?

26 During the time when Abiathar was high priest, David went into God's house and ate the bread of the presence, which only the priests were allowed to eat. He also gave bread to those who were with him."

27 Then he said, "The Sabbath was created for humans; humans weren't created for the Sabbath.

28 This is why the Human One is Lord even over the Sabbath."

Key words or phrases?

Insights?

Mark 3:1-6

1 Jesus returned to the synagogue. A man with a withered hand was there.

2 Wanting to bring charges against Jesus, they were watching Jesus closely to see if he would heal on the Sabbath.

3 He said to the man with the withered hand, "Step up where people can see you."

4 Then he said to them, "Is it legal on the Sabbath to do good or to do evil, to save life or to kill?" But they said nothing.

5 Looking around at them with anger, deeply grieved at their unyielding hearts, he said to the man, "Stretch out your hand." So he did, and his hand was made healthy.

6 At that, the Pharisees got together with the supporters of Herod to plan how to destroy Jesus.

Key words or phrases?

Insights?

Mark 4:1-9, 13-20

¹ Jesus began to teach beside the lake again. Such a large crowd gathered that he climbed into a boat there on the lake. He sat in the boat while the whole crowd was nearby on the shore.

² He said many things to them in parables. While teaching them, he said, ³ "Listen to this! A farmer went out to scatter seed.

⁴ As he was scattering seed, some fell on the path; and the birds came and ate it.

⁵ Other seed fell on rocky ground where the soil was shallow. They sprouted immediately because the soil wasn't deep.

⁶ When the sun came up, it scorched the plants; and they dried up because they had no roots.

⁷ Other seed fell among thorny plants. The thorny plants grew and choked the seeds, and they produced nothing.

⁸ Other seed fell into good soil and bore fruit. Upon growing and increasing, the seed produced in one case a yield of thirty to one, in another case a yield of sixty to one, and in another case a yield of one hundred to one."

⁹ He said, "Whoever has ears to listen should pay attention!"

¹³ "Don't you understand this parable? Then how will you understand all the parables?

¹⁴ The farmer scatters the word.

15 This is the meaning of the seed that fell on the path: When the word is scattered and people hear it, right away Satan comes and steals the word that was planted in them.

16 Here's the meaning of the seed that fell on rocky ground: When people hear the word, they immediately receive it joyfully.

17 Because they have no roots, they last for only a little while. When they experience distress or abuse because of the word, they immediately fall away.

18 Others are like the seed scattered among the thorny plants. These are the ones who have heard the word; 19 but the worries of this life, the false appeal of wealth, and the desire for more things break in and choke the word, and it bears no fruit.

20 The seed scattered on good soil are those who hear the word and embrace it. They bear fruit, in one case a yield of thirty to one, in another case sixty to one, and in another case one hundred to one."

Key words or phrases?

Insights?

Mark 4:21-34

21 Jesus said to them, "Does anyone bring in a lamp in order to put it under a basket or a bed? Shouldn't it be placed on a lampstand?

22 Everything hidden will be revealed, and everything secret will come out into the open.

23 Whoever has ears to listen should pay attention!"

24 He said to them, "Listen carefully! God will evaluate you with the same standard you use to evaluate others. Indeed, you will receive even more.

25 Those who have will receive more, but as for those who don't have, even what they don't have will be taken away from them."

26 Then Jesus said, "This is what God's kingdom is like. It's as though someone scatters seed on the ground, 27 then sleeps and wakes night and day. The seed sprouts and grows, but the farmer doesn't know how.

28 The earth produces crops all by itself, first the stalk, then the head, then the full head of grain.

29 Whenever the crop is ready, the farmer goes out to cut the grain because it's harvesttime."

30 He continued, "What's a good image for God's kingdom? What parable can I use to explain it?

31 Consider a mustard seed. When scattered on the ground, it's the smallest of all the seeds on the earth; 32 but when it's planted, it grows and becomes the largest of all vegetable plants. It produces such large branches that the birds in the sky are able to nest in its shade."

33 With many such parables he continued to give them the word, as much as they were able to hear.

34 He spoke to them only in parables, then explained everything to his disciples when he was alone with them.

Key words or phrases?

Insights?

Mark 4:35-41

35 Later that day, when evening came, Jesus said to them, "Let's cross over to the other side of the lake."

36 They left the crowd and took him in the boat just as he was. Other boats followed along.

37 Gale-force winds arose, and waves crashed against the boat so that the boat was swamped.

38 But Jesus was in the rear of the boat, sleeping on a pillow. They woke him up and said, "Teacher, don't you care that we're drowning?"

39 He got up and gave orders to the wind, and he said to the lake, "Silence! Be still!" The wind settled down and there was a great calm.

40 Jesus asked them, "Why are you frightened? Don't you have faith yet?"

41 Overcome with awe, they said to each other, "Who then is this? Even the wind and the sea obey him!"

Key words or phrases?

Insights?

Mark 5:21-24, 35-43

21 Jesus crossed the lake again, and on the other side a large crowd gathered around him on the shore.

22 Jairus, one of the synagogue leaders, came forward. When he saw Jesus, he fell at his feet 23 and pleaded with him, "My daughter is about to die. Please, come and place your hands on her so that she can be healed and live."

24 So Jesus went with him.

35 While Jesus was still speaking with her, messengers came from the synagogue leader's house, saying to Jairus, "Your daughter has died. Why bother the teacher any longer?"

36 But Jesus overheard their report and said to the synagogue leader, "Don't be afraid; just keep trusting."

37 He didn't allow anyone to follow him except Peter, James, and John, James' brother.

38 They came to the synagogue leader's house, and he saw a commotion, with people crying and wailing loudly.

39 He went in and said to them, "What's all this commotion and crying about? The child isn't dead. She's only sleeping."

40 They laughed at him, but he threw them all out. Then, taking the child's parents and his disciples with him, he went to the room where the child was.

41 Taking her hand, he said to her, "Talitha koum," which means, "Young woman, get up."

42 Suddenly the young woman got up and began to walk around. She was 12 years old. They were shocked!

43 He gave them strict orders that no one should know what had happened. Then he told them to give her something to eat.

Key words or phrases?

Insights?

Mark 6:30-44

30 The apostles returned to Jesus and told him everything they had done and taught.

31 Many people were coming and going, so there was no time to eat. He said to the apostles, "Come by yourselves to a secluded place and rest for a while."

32 They departed in a boat by themselves for a deserted place.

33 Many people saw them leaving and recognized them, so they ran ahead from all the cities and arrived before them.

34 When Jesus arrived and saw a large crowd, he had compassion on them because they were like sheep without a shepherd. Then he began to teach them many things.

35 Late in the day, his disciples came to him and said, "This is an isolated place, and it's already late in the day.

36 Send them away so that they can go to the surrounding countryside and villages and buy something to eat for themselves."

37 He replied, "You give them something to eat." But they said to him, "Should we go off and buy bread worth almost eight months' pay and give it to them to eat?"

38 He said to them, "How much bread do you have? Take a look." After checking, they said, "Five loaves of bread and two fish."

39 He directed the disciples to seat all the people in groups as though they were having a banquet on the green grass.

40 They sat down in groups of hundreds and fifties.

41 He took the five loaves and the two fish, looked up to heaven, blessed them, broke the loaves into pieces, and gave them to his disciples to set before the people. He also divided the two fish among them all.

42 Everyone ate until they were full.

43 They filled twelve baskets with the leftover pieces of bread and fish.

44 About five thousand had eaten.

Key words or phrases?

Insights?

Mark 7:1-13

1 The Pharisees and some legal experts from Jerusalem gathered around Jesus.

2 They saw some of his disciples eating food with unclean hands. (They were eating without first ritually purifying their hands through washing.

3 The Pharisees and all the Jews don't eat without first washing their hands carefully. This is a way of observing the rules handed down by the elders.

4 Upon returning from the marketplace, they don't eat without first immersing themselves. They observe many other rules that have been handed down, such as the washing of cups, jugs, pans, and sleeping mats.)

5 So the Pharisees and legal experts asked Jesus, "Why are your disciples not living according to the rules handed down by the elders but instead eat food with ritually unclean hands?"

6 He replied, "Isaiah really knew what he was talking about when he prophesied about you hypocrites. He wrote,

> This people honors me with their lips,
>   but their hearts are far away from me.
7 Their worship of me is empty
since they teach instructions that are human words.
[Isaiah 29:13]

8 You ignore God's commandment while holding on to rules created by humans and handed down to you."

⁹ Jesus continued, "Clearly, you are experts at rejecting God's commandment in order to establish these rules.

¹⁰ Moses said, Honor your father and your mother, and The person who speaks against father or mother will certainly be put to death.

¹¹ But you say, 'If you tell your father or mother, "Everything I'm expected to contribute to you is corban (that is, a gift I'm giving to God)," ¹² then you are no longer required to care for your father or mother.'

¹³ In this way you do away with God's word in favor of the rules handed down to you, which you pass on to others. And you do a lot of other things just like that."

Key words or phrases?

Insights?

Mark 7:14-23

¹⁴ Then Jesus called the crowd again and said, "Listen to me, all of you, and understand.

¹⁵ Nothing outside of a person can enter and contaminate a person in God's sight; rather, the things that come out of a person contaminate the person."

¹⁷ After leaving the crowd, he entered a house where his disciples asked him about that riddle.

¹⁸ He said to them, "Don't you understand either? Don't you know that nothing from the outside that enters a person has the power to contaminate?

¹⁹ That's because it doesn't enter into the heart but into the stomach, and it goes out into the sewer." By saying this, Jesus declared that no food could contaminate a person in God's sight.

²⁰ "It's what comes out of a person that contaminates someone in God's sight," he said.

²¹ "It's from the inside, from the human heart, that evil thoughts come: sexual sins, thefts, murders, ²² adultery, greed, evil actions, deceit, unrestrained immorality, envy, insults, arrogance, and foolishness.

²³ All these evil things come from the inside and contaminate a person in God's sight."

Key words or phrases?

Insights?

Mark 7:31-37

³¹ After leaving the region of Tyre, Jesus went through Sidon toward the Galilee Sea through the region of the Ten Cities.

³² Some people brought to him a man who was deaf and could hardly speak, and they begged him to place his hand on the man for healing.

³³ Jesus took him away from the crowd by himself and put his fingers in the man's ears. Then he spit and touched the man's tongue.

³⁴ Looking into heaven, Jesus sighed deeply and said, "Ephphatha," which means, "Open up."

³⁵ At once, his ears opened, his twisted tongue was released, and he began to speak clearly.

³⁶ Jesus gave the people strict orders not to tell anyone. But the more he tried to silence them, the more eagerly they shared the news.

³⁷ People were overcome with wonder, saying, "He does everything well! He even makes the deaf to hear and gives speech to those who can't speak."

Key words or phrases?

Insights?

Mark 8:1-10

1 In those days there was another large crowd with nothing to eat. Jesus called his disciples and told them, 2 "I feel sorry for the crowd because they have been with me for three days and have nothing to eat.

3 If I send them away hungry to their homes, they won't have enough strength to travel, for some have come a long distance."

4 His disciples responded, "How can anyone get enough food in this wilderness to satisfy these people?"

5 Jesus asked, "How much bread do you have?" They said, "Seven loaves."

6 He told the crowd to sit on the ground. He took the seven loaves, gave thanks, broke them apart, and gave them to his disciples to distribute; and they gave the bread to the crowd.

7 They also had a few fish. He said a blessing over them, then gave them to the disciples to hand out also.

8 They ate until they were full. They collected seven baskets full of leftovers.

9 This was a crowd of about four thousand people! Jesus sent them away, 10 then got into a boat with his disciples and went over to the region of Dalmanutha.

Key words or phrases?

Insights?

Mark 8:22-26

22 Jesus and his disciples came to Bethsaida. Some people brought a blind man to Jesus and begged him to touch and heal him.

23 Taking the blind man's hand, Jesus led him out of the village. After spitting on his eyes and laying his hands on the man, he asked him, "Do you see anything?"

24 The man looked up and said, "I see people. They look like trees, only they are walking around."

25 Then Jesus placed his hands on the man's eyes again. He looked with his eyes wide open, his sight was restored, and he could see everything clearly.

26 Then Jesus sent him home, saying, "Don't go into the village!"

Key words or phrases?

Insights?

Mark 8:27-38

²⁷ Jesus and his disciples went into the villages near Caesarea Philippi. On the way he asked his disciples, "Who do people say that I am?"

²⁸ They told him, "Some say John the Baptist, others Elijah, and still others one of the prophets."

²⁹ He asked them, "And what about you? Who do you say that I am?" Peter answered, "You are the Christ."

³⁰ Jesus ordered them not to tell anyone about him.

³¹ Then Jesus began to teach his disciples: "The Human One must suffer many things and be rejected by the elders, chief priests, and the legal experts, and be killed, and then, after three days, rise from the dead."

³² He said this plainly. But Peter took hold of Jesus and, scolding him, began to correct him.

³³ Jesus turned and looked at his disciples, then sternly corrected Peter: "Get behind me, Satan. You are not thinking God's thoughts but human thoughts."

³⁴ After calling the crowd together with his disciples, Jesus said to them, "All who want to come after me must say no to themselves, take up their cross, and follow me.

³⁵ All who want to save their lives will lose them. But all who lose their lives because of me and because of the good news will save them.

³⁶ Why would people gain the whole world but lose their lives?

³⁷ What will people give in exchange for their lives?

³⁸ Whoever is ashamed of me and my words in this unfaithful and sinful generation, the Human One will be ashamed of that person when he comes in the Father's glory with the holy angels."

Key words or phrases?

Insights?

Mark 9:2-10

2 Six days later Jesus took Peter, James, and John, and brought them to the top of a very high mountain where they were alone. He was transformed in front of them, ³ and his clothes were amazingly bright, brighter than if they had been bleached white.

4 Elijah and Moses appeared and were talking with Jesus.

5 Peter reacted to all of this by saying to Jesus, "Rabbi, it's good that we're here. Let's make three shrines—one for you, one for Moses, and one for Elijah."

6 He said this because he didn't know how to respond, for the three of them were terrified.

7 Then a cloud overshadowed them, and a voice spoke from the cloud, "This is my Son, whom I dearly love. Listen to him!"

8 Suddenly, looking around, they no longer saw anyone with them except Jesus.

9 As they were coming down the mountain, he ordered them not to tell anyone what they had seen until after the Human One had risen from the dead.

10 So they kept it to themselves, wondering, "What's this 'rising from the dead'?"

Key words or phrases?

Insights?

Mark 9:14-29

14 When Jesus, Peter, James, and John approached the other disciples, they saw a large crowd surrounding them and legal experts arguing with them.

15 Suddenly the whole crowd caught sight of Jesus. They ran to greet him, overcome with excitement.

16 Jesus asked them, "What are you arguing about?"

17 Someone from the crowd responded, "Teacher, I brought my son to you, since he has a spirit that doesn't allow him to speak.

18 Wherever it overpowers him, it throws him into a fit. He foams at the mouth, grinds his teeth, and stiffens up. So I spoke to your disciples to see if they could throw it out, but they couldn't."

19 Jesus answered them, "You faithless generation, how long will I be with you? How long will I put up with you? Bring him to me."

20 They brought him. When the spirit saw Jesus, it immediately threw the boy into a fit. He fell on the ground and rolled around, foaming at the mouth.

21 Jesus asked his father, "How long has this been going on?"

He said, "Since he was a child. 22 It has often thrown him into a fire or into water trying to kill him. If you can do anything, help us! Show us compassion!"

23 Jesus said to him, "'If you can do anything'? All things are possible for the one who has faith."

24 At that the boy's father cried out, "I have faith; help my lack of faith!"

25 Noticing that the crowd had surged together, Jesus spoke harshly to the unclean spirit, "Mute and deaf spirit, I command you to come out of him and never enter him again."

26 After screaming and shaking the boy horribly, the spirit came out. The boy seemed to be dead; in fact, several people said that he had died.

27 But Jesus took his hand, lifted him up, and he arose.

28 After Jesus went into a house, his disciples asked him privately, "Why couldn't we throw this spirit out?"

29 Jesus answered, "Throwing this kind of spirit out requires prayer."

Key words or phrases?

Insights?

Mark 9:33-37, 42-43, 45, 47-49

33 They entered Capernaum. When they had come into a house, he asked them, "What were you arguing about during the journey?"

34 They didn't respond, since on the way they had been debating with each other about who was the greatest.

35 He sat down, called the Twelve, and said to them, "Whoever wants to be first must be least of all and the servant of all."

36 Jesus reached for a little child, placed him among the Twelve, and embraced him. Then he said,

37 "Whoever welcomes one of these children in my name welcomes me; and whoever welcomes me isn't actually welcoming me but rather the one who sent me."

42 "As for whoever causes these little ones who believe in me to trip and fall into sin, it would be better for them to have a huge stone hung around their necks and to be thrown into the lake.

43 If your hand causes you to fall into sin, chop it off. It's better for you to enter into life crippled than to go away with two hands into the fire of hell, which can't be put out.

45 If your foot causes you to fall into sin, chop it off. It's better for you to enter life lame than to be thrown into hell with two feet.

47 If your eye causes you to fall into sin, tear it out. It's better for you to enter God's kingdom with one eye than to be thrown into hell with two.

48 That's a place where worms don't die and the fire never goes out.

49 Everyone will be salted with fire.

Key words or phrases?

Insights?

Mark 10:17-31

17 As Jesus continued down the road, a man ran up, knelt before him, and asked, "Good Teacher, what must I do to obtain eternal life?"

18 Jesus replied, "Why do you call me good? No one is good except the one God.

19 You know the commandments: Don't commit murder. Don't commit adultery. Don't steal. Don't give false testimony. Don't cheat. Honor your father and mother."

20 "Teacher," he responded, "I've kept all of these things since I was a boy."

21 Jesus looked at him carefully and loved him. He said, "You are lacking one thing. Go, sell what you own, and give the money to the poor. Then you will have treasure in heaven. And come, follow me."

22 But the man was dismayed at this statement and went away saddened, because he had many possessions.

23 Looking around, Jesus said to his disciples, "It will be very hard for the wealthy to enter God's kingdom!"

24 His words startled the disciples, so Jesus told them again, "Children, it's difficult to enter God's kingdom!

25 It's easier for a camel to squeeze through the eye of a needle than for a rich person to enter God's kingdom."

26 They were shocked even more and said to each other, "Then who can be saved?"

27 Jesus looked at them carefully and said, "It's impossible with human beings, but not with God. All things are possible for God."

28 Peter said to him, "Look, we've left everything and followed you."

29 Jesus said, "I assure you that anyone who has left house, brothers, sisters, mother, father, children, or farms because of me and because of the good news 30 will receive one hundred times as much now in this life—houses, brothers, sisters, mothers, children, and farms (with harassment)—and in the coming age, eternal life.

31 But many who are first will be last. And many who are last will be first."

Key words or phrases?

Insights?

Mark 10:35-45

35 James and John, Zebedee's sons, came to Jesus and said, "Teacher, we want you to do for us whatever we ask."

36 "What do you want me to do for you?" he asked.

37 They said, "Allow one of us to sit on your right and the other on your left when you enter your glory."

38 Jesus replied, "You don't know what you're asking! Can you drink the cup I drink or receive the baptism I receive?"

39 "We can," they answered. Jesus said, "You will drink the cup I drink and receive the baptism I receive, 40 but to sit at my right or left hand isn't mine to give. It belongs to those for whom it has been prepared."

41 Now when the other ten disciples heard about this, they became angry with James and John.

42 Jesus called them over and said, "You know that the ones who are considered the rulers by the Gentiles show off their authority over them and their high-ranking officials order them around.

43 But that's not the way it will be with you. Whoever wants to be great among you will be your servant.

44 Whoever wants to be first among you will be the slave of all, 45 for the Human One didn't come to be served but rather to serve and to give his life to liberate many people."

Key words or phrases?

Insights?

Mark 10:46-52

⁴⁶ Jesus and his followers came into Jericho. As Jesus was leaving Jericho, together with his disciples and a sizable crowd, a blind beggar named Bartimaeus, Timaeus' son, was sitting beside the road.

⁴⁷ When he heard that Jesus of Nazareth was there, he began to shout, "Jesus, Son of David, show me mercy!"

⁴⁸ Many scolded him, telling him to be quiet, but he shouted even louder, "Son of David, show me mercy!"

⁴⁹ Jesus stopped and said, "Call him forward." They called the blind man, "Be encouraged! Get up! He's calling you."

⁵⁰ Throwing his coat to the side, he jumped up and came to Jesus.

⁵¹ Jesus asked him, "What do you want me to do for you?" The blind man said, "Teacher, I want to see."

⁵² Jesus said, "Go, your faith has healed you." At once he was able to see, and he began to follow Jesus on the way.

Key words or phrases?

Insights?

Mark 11:1-11

1 When Jesus and his followers approached Jerusalem, they came to Bethphage and Bethany at the Mount of Olives. Jesus gave two disciples a task, 2 saying to them, "Go into the village over there. As soon as you enter it, you will find tied up there a colt that no one has ridden. Untie it and bring it here.

3 If anyone says to you, 'Why are you doing this?' say, 'Its master needs it, and he will send it back right away.'"

4 They went and found a colt tied to a gate outside on the street, and they untied it.

5 Some people standing around said to them, "What are you doing, untying the colt?"

6 They told them just what Jesus said, and they left them alone.

7 They brought the colt to Jesus and threw their clothes upon it, and he sat on it.

8 Many people spread out their clothes on the road while others spread branches cut from the fields.

9 Those in front of him and those following were shouting, "Hosanna! Blessings on the one who comes in the name of the Lord!

10 Blessings on the coming kingdom of our ancestor David! Hosanna in the highest!"

11 Jesus entered Jerusalem and went into the temple. After he looked around at everything, because it was already late in the evening, he returned to Bethany with the Twelve.

Key words or phrases?

Insights?

Mark 11:15-19

15 They came into Jerusalem. After entering the temple, he threw out those who were selling and buying there. He pushed over the tables used for currency exchange and the chairs of those who sold doves.

16 He didn't allow anyone to carry anything through the temple.

17 He taught them, "Hasn't it been written, My house will be called a house of prayer for all nations? But you've turned it into a hideout for crooks."

18 The chief priests and legal experts heard this and tried to find a way to destroy him. They regarded him as dangerous because the whole crowd was enthralled at his teaching.

19 When it was evening, Jesus and his disciples went outside the city.

Key words or phrases?

Insights?

Mark 12:1-12

1 Jesus spoke to them in parables. "A man planted a vineyard, put a fence around it, dug a pit for the winepress, and built a tower. Then he rented it to tenant farmers and took a trip.

2 When it was time, he sent a servant to collect from the tenants his share of the fruit of the vineyard.

3 But they grabbed the servant, beat him, and sent him away empty-handed.

4 Again the landowner sent another servant to them, but they struck him on the head and treated him disgracefully.

5 He sent another one; that one they killed. The landlord sent many other servants, but the tenants beat some and killed others.

6 Now the landowner had one son whom he loved dearly. He sent him last, thinking, They will respect my son.

7 But those tenant farmers said to each other, 'This is the heir. Let's kill him, and the inheritance will be ours.'

8 They grabbed him, killed him, and threw him out of the vineyard.

9 "So what will the owner of the vineyard do? He will come and destroy those tenants and give the vineyard to others.

10 Haven't you read this scripture, The stone that the builders rejected has become the cornerstone.

11 The Lord has done this, and it's amazing in our eyes?"

12 They wanted to arrest Jesus because they knew that he had told the parable against them. But they were afraid of the crowd, so they left him and went away.

Key words or phrases?

Insights?

Mark 12:13-17

13 They sent some of the Pharisees and supporters of Herod to trap him in his words.

14 They came to him and said, "Teacher, we know that you're genuine and you don't worry about what people think. You don't show favoritism but teach God's way as it really is. Does the Law allow people to pay taxes to Caesar or not? Should we pay taxes or not?"

15 Since Jesus recognized their deceit, he said to them, "Why are you testing me? Bring me a coin. Show it to me."

16 And they brought one. He said to them, "Whose image and inscription is this?" "Caesar's," they replied.

17 Jesus said to them, "Give to Caesar what belongs to Caesar and to God what belongs to God." His reply left them overcome with wonder.

Key words or phrases?

Insights?

Mark 12:28-34

28 One of the legal experts heard their dispute and saw how well Jesus answered them. He came over and asked him, "Which commandment is the most important of all?"

29 Jesus replied, "The most important one is Israel, listen! Our God is the one Lord, 30 and you must love the Lord your God with all your heart, with all your being, with all your mind, and with all your strength.

31 The second is this, You will love your neighbor as yourself. No other commandment is greater than these."

32 The legal expert said to him, "Well said, Teacher. You have truthfully said that God is one and there is no other besides him.

33 And to love God with all of the heart, a full understanding, and all of one's strength, and to love one's neighbor as oneself is much more important than all kinds of entirely burned offerings and sacrifices."

34 When Jesus saw that he had answered with wisdom, he said to him, "You aren't far from God's kingdom." After that, no one dared to ask him any more questions.

Key words or phrases?

Insights?

Mark 12:38-44

³⁸ As he was teaching, he said, "Watch out for the legal experts. They like to walk around in long robes. They want to be greeted with honor in the markets.

³⁹ They long for places of honor in the synagogues and at banquets.

⁴⁰ They are the ones who cheat widows out of their homes, and to show off they say long prayers. They will be judged most harshly."

⁴¹ Jesus sat across from the collection box for the temple treasury and observed how the crowd gave their money. Many rich people were throwing in lots of money.

⁴² One poor widow came forward and put in two small copper coins worth a penny.

⁴³ Jesus called his disciples to him and said, "I assure you that this poor widow has put in more than everyone who's been putting money in the treasury.

⁴⁴ All of them are giving out of their spare change. But she from her hopeless poverty has given everything she had, even what she needed to live on."

Key words or phrases?

Insights?

Mark 13:28-37

28 "Learn this parable from the fig tree. After its branch becomes tender and it sprouts new leaves, you know that summer is near.

29 In the same way, when you see these things happening, you know that he's near, at the door.

30 I assure you that this generation won't pass away until all these things happen.

31 Heaven and earth will pass away, but my words will certainly not pass away.

32 "But nobody knows when that day or hour will come, not the angels in heaven and not the Son. Only the Father knows.

33 Watch out! Stay alert! You don't know when the time is coming.

34 It is as if someone took a trip, left the household behind, and put the servants in charge, giving each one a job to do, and told the doorkeeper to stay alert.

35 Therefore, stay alert! You don't know when the head of the household will come, whether in the evening or at midnight, or when the rooster crows in the early morning or at daybreak.

36 Don't let him show up when you weren't expecting and find you sleeping.

37 What I say to you, I say to all: Stay alert!"

Key words or phrases?

Insights?

Mark 14:3-9

³ Jesus was at Bethany visiting the house of Simon, who had a skin disease. During dinner, a woman came in with a vase made of alabaster and containing very expensive perfume of pure nard. She broke open the vase and poured the perfume on his head.

⁴ Some grew angry. They said to each other, "Why waste the perfume?

⁵ This perfume could have been sold for almost a year's pay and the money given to the poor." And they scolded her.

⁶ Jesus said, "Leave her alone. Why do you make trouble for her? She has done a good thing for me.

⁷ You always have the poor with you; and whenever you want, you can do something good for them. But you won't always have me.

⁸ She has done what she could. She has anointed my body ahead of time for burial.

⁹ I tell you the truth that, wherever in the whole world the good news is announced, what she's done will also be told in memory of her."

Key words or phrases?

Insights?

Mark 14:12-26

12 On the first day of the Festival of Unleavened Bread, when the Passover lamb was sacrificed, the disciples said to Jesus, "Where do you want us to prepare for you to eat the Passover meal?"

13 He sent two of his disciples and said to them, "Go into the city. A man carrying a water jar will meet you. Follow him.

14 Wherever he enters, say to the owner of the house, 'The teacher asks, "Where is my guest room where I can eat the Passover meal with my disciples?" '

15 He will show you a large room upstairs already furnished. Prepare for us there."

16 The disciples left, came into the city, found everything just as he had told them, and they prepared the Passover meal.

17 That evening, Jesus arrived with the Twelve.

18 During the meal, Jesus said, "I assure you that one of you will betray me—someone eating with me."

19 Deeply saddened, they asked him, one by one, "It's not me, is it?"

20 Jesus answered, "It's one of the Twelve, one who is dipping bread with me into this bowl.

21 The Human One goes to his death just as it is written about him. But how terrible it is for that person who betrays the Human One! It would have been better for him if he had never been born."

²² While they were eating, Jesus took bread, blessed it, broke it, and gave it to them, and said, "Take; this is my body."

²³ He took a cup, gave thanks, and gave it to them, and they all drank from it.

²⁴ He said to them, "This is my blood of the covenant, which is poured out for many.

²⁵ I assure you that I won't drink wine again until that day when I drink it in a new way in God's kingdom."

²⁶ After singing songs of praise, they went out to the Mount of Olives.

Key words or phrases?

Insights?

Mark 14:32-42

32 Jesus and his disciples came to a place called Gethsemane. Jesus said to them, "Sit here while I pray."

33 He took Peter, James, and John along with him. He began to feel despair and was anxious.

34 He said to them, "I'm very sad. It's as if I'm dying. Stay here and keep alert."

35 Then he went a short distance farther and fell to the ground. He prayed that, if possible, he might be spared the time of suffering.

36 He said, "Abba, Father, for you all things are possible. Take this cup of suffering away from me. However—not what I want but what you want."

37 He came and found them sleeping. He said to Peter, "Simon, are you asleep? Couldn't you stay alert for one hour?

38 Stay alert and pray so that you won't give in to temptation. The spirit is eager, but the flesh is weak."

39 Again, he left them and prayed, repeating the same words.

40 And, again, when he came back, he found them sleeping, for they couldn't keep their eyes open, and they didn't know how to respond to him.

41 He came a third time and said to them, "Will you sleep and rest all night? That's enough! The time has come for the Human One[e] to be betrayed into the hands of sinners.

42 Get up! Let's go! Look, here comes my betrayer."

Key words or phrases?

Insights?

Mark 14:52-65

53 They led Jesus away to the high priest, and all the chief priests, elders, and legal experts gathered.

54 Peter followed him from a distance, right into the high priest's courtyard. He was sitting with the guards, warming himself by the fire.

55 The chief priests and the whole Sanhedrin were looking for testimony against Jesus in order to put him to death, but they couldn't find any.

56 Many brought false testimony against him, but they contradicted each other.

57 Some stood to offer false witness against him, saying, 58 "We heard him saying, 'I will destroy this temple, constructed by humans, and within three days I will build another, one not made by humans.'"

59 But their testimonies didn't agree even on this point.

60 Then the high priest stood up in the middle of the gathering and examined Jesus. "Aren't you going to respond to the testimony these people have brought against you?"

61 But Jesus was silent and didn't answer. Again, the high priest asked, "Are you the Christ, the Son of the blessed one?"

62 Jesus said, "I am. And you will see the Human One sitting on the right side of the Almighty and coming on the heavenly clouds."

63 Then the high priest tore his clothes and said, "Why do we need any more witnesses?

64 You've heard his insult against God. What do you think?" They all condemned him. "He deserves to die!"

65 Some began to spit on him. Some covered his face and hit him, saying, "Prophesy!" Then the guards took him and beat him.

Key words or phrases?

Insights?

Mark 14:27-31, 66-72

27 Jesus said to them, "You will all falter in your faithfulness to me. It is written, I will hit the shepherd, and the sheep will go off in all directions.

28 But after I'm raised up, I will go before you to Galilee."

29 Peter said to him, "Even if everyone else stumbles, I won't."

30 But Jesus said to him, "I assure you that on this very night, before the rooster crows twice, you will deny me three times."

31 But Peter insisted, "If I must die alongside you, I won't deny you." And they all said the same thing.

66 Meanwhile, Peter was below in the courtyard. A woman, one of the high priest's servants, approached 67 and saw Peter warming himself by the fire. She stared at him and said, "You were also with the Nazarene, Jesus."

68 But he denied it, saying, "I don't know what you're talking about. I don't understand what you're saying." And he went outside into the outer courtyard. A rooster crowed.

69 The female servant saw him and began a second time to say to those standing around, "This man is one of them."

70 But he denied it again. A short time later, those standing around again said to Peter, "You must be one of them, because you are also a Galilean."

71 But he cursed and swore, "I don't know this man you're talking about."

72 At that very moment, a rooster crowed a second time. Peter remembered what Jesus told him, "Before a rooster crows twice, you will deny me three times." And he broke down, sobbing.

Key words or phrases?

Insights?

Mark 15:6-15, 21-32

⁶ During the festival, Pilate released one prisoner to them, whomever they requested.

⁷ A man named Barabbas was locked up with the rebels who had committed murder during an uprising.

⁸ The crowd pushed forward and asked Pilate to release someone, as he regularly did.

⁹ Pilate answered them, "Do you want me to release to you the king of the Jews?"

¹⁰ He knew that the chief priests had handed him over because of jealousy.

¹¹ But the chief priests stirred up the crowd to have him release Barabbas to them instead.

¹² Pilate replied, "Then what do you want me to do with the one you call king of the Jews?"

¹³ They shouted back, "Crucify him!"

¹⁴ Pilate said to them, "Why? What wrong has he done?" They shouted even louder, "Crucify him!"

¹⁵ Pilate wanted to satisfy the crowd, so he released Barabbas to them. He had Jesus whipped, then handed him over to be crucified.

21 Simon, a man from Cyrene, Alexander and Rufus' father, was coming in from the countryside. They forced him to carry his cross.

22 They brought Jesus to the place called Golgotha, which means Skull Place.

23 They tried to give him wine mixed with myrrh, but he didn't take it.

24 They crucified him. They divided up his clothes, drawing lots for them to determine who would take what.

25 It was nine in the morning when they crucified him.

26 The notice of the formal charge against him was written, "The king of the Jews."

27 They crucified two outlaws with him, one on his right and one on his left.

29 People walking by insulted him, shaking their heads and saying, "Ha! So you were going to destroy the temple and rebuild it in three days, were you?

30 Save yourself and come down from that cross!"

31 In the same way, the chief priests were making fun of him among themselves, together with the legal experts. "He saved others," they said, "but he can't save himself.

32 Let the Christ, the king of Israel, come down from the cross. Then we'll see and believe." Even those who had been crucified with Jesus insulted him.

Key words or phrases?

Insights?

Mark 15:33-41

³³ From noon until three in the afternoon the whole earth was dark.

³⁴ At three, Jesus cried out with a loud shout, "Eloi, eloi, lama sabachthani," which means, "My God, my God, why have you left me?"

³⁵ After hearing him, some standing there said, "Look! He's calling Elijah!"

³⁶ Someone ran, filled a sponge with sour wine, and put it on a pole. He offered it to Jesus to drink, saying, "Let's see if Elijah will come to take him down."

³⁷ But Jesus let out a loud cry and died.

³⁸ The curtain of the sanctuary was torn in two from top to bottom.

³⁹ When the centurion, who stood facing Jesus, saw how he died, he said, "This man was certainly God's Son."

⁴⁰ Some women were watching from a distance, including Mary Magdalene and Mary the mother of James (the younger one) and Joses, and Salome.

⁴¹ When Jesus was in Galilee, these women had followed and supported him, along with many other women who had come to Jerusalem with him.

⁴² Since it was late in the afternoon on Preparation Day, just before the Sabbath, ⁴³ Joseph from Arimathea dared to approach Pilate and ask for Jesus' body. (Joseph was a prominent council member who also eagerly anticipated the coming of God's kingdom.)

⁴⁴ Pilate wondered if Jesus was already dead. He called the centurion and asked him whether Jesus had already died.

⁴⁵ When he learned from the centurion that Jesus was dead, Pilate gave the dead body to Joseph.

⁴⁶ He bought a linen cloth, took Jesus down from the cross, wrapped him in the cloth, and laid him in a tomb that had been carved out of rock. He rolled a stone against the entrance to the tomb.

⁴⁷ Mary Magdalene and Mary the mother of Joses saw where he was buried.

Key words or phrases?

Insights?

Mark 15:42-16:8

1 When the Sabbath was over, Mary Magdalene, Mary the mother of James, and Salome bought spices so that they could go and anoint Jesus' dead body.

2 Very early on the first day of the week, just after sunrise, they came to the tomb.

3 They were saying to each other, "Who's going to roll the stone away from the entrance for us?"

4 When they looked up, they saw that the stone had been rolled away. (And it was a very large stone!)

5 Going into the tomb, they saw a young man in a white robe seated on the right side; and they were startled.

6 But he said to them, "Don't be alarmed! You are looking for Jesus of Nazareth, who was crucified. He has been raised. He isn't here. Look, here's the place where they laid him.

7 Go, tell his disciples, especially Peter, that he is going ahead of you into Galilee. You will see him there, just as he told you."

8 Overcome with terror and dread, they fled from the tomb. They said nothing to anyone, because they were afraid.

Key words or phrases?

Insights?

Mark 16:9-20

9 After Jesus rose up early on the first day of the week, he appeared first to Mary Magdalene, from whom he had cast out seven demons.

10 She went and reported to the ones who had been with him, who were mourning and weeping.

11 But even after they heard the news, they didn't believe that Jesus was alive and that Mary had seen him.

12 After that he appeared in a different form to two of them who were walking along in the countryside.

13 When they returned, they reported it to the others, but they didn't believe them.

14 Finally he appeared to the eleven while they were eating. Jesus criticized their unbelief and stubbornness because they didn't believe those who saw him after he was raised up.

15 He said to them, "Go into the whole world and proclaim the good news to every creature.

16 Whoever believes and is baptized will be saved, but whoever doesn't believe will be condemned.

17 These signs will be associated with those who believe: they will throw out demons in my name. They will speak in new languages.

18 They will pick up snakes with their hands. If they drink anything poisonous, it will not hurt them. They will place their hands on the sick, and they will get well."

19 After the Lord Jesus spoke to them, he was lifted up into heaven and sat down on the right side of God.

20 But they went out and proclaimed the message everywhere. The Lord worked with them, confirming the word by the signs associated with them.

Key words or phrases?

Insights?

95879103R00070

Made in the USA
Columbia, SC
24 May 2018